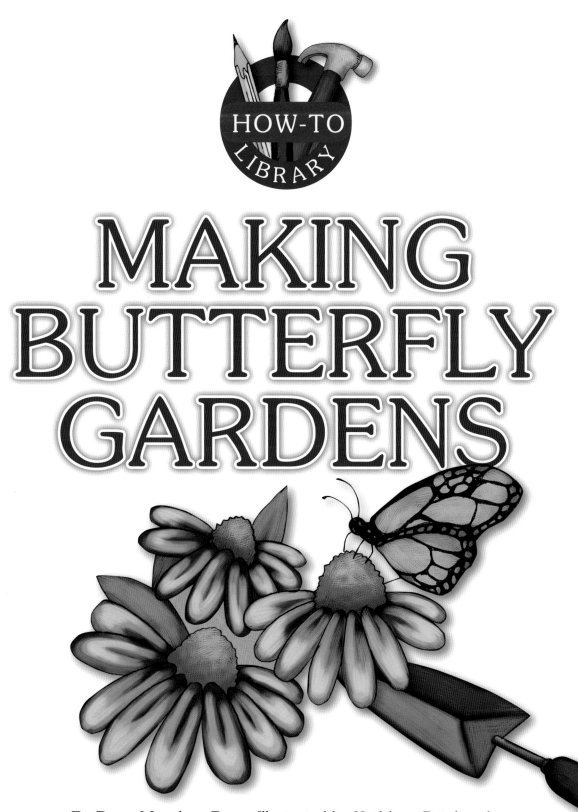

MAKING BUTTERFLY GARDENS

By Dana Meachen Rau • Illustrated by Kathleen Petelinsek

CHERRY LAKE PUBLISHING • ANN ARBOR, MICHIGAN

CHERRY LAKE

Publishing

Published in the United States of America by Cherry Lake Publishing
Ann Arbor, Michigan
www.cherrylakepublishing.com

Content Adviser: Dr. Julia L. Hovanec, Professor of Art Education, Kutztown University, Kutztown, Pennsylvania

Photo Credits: Page 4, ©chanwangrong/Shutterstock, Inc.; page 5 top, ©Le Do/Shutterstock, Inc.; page 5 bottom, ©Mikhail Melnikov/Shutterstock, Inc.; page 8, ©Willyam Bradberry/Shutterstock, Inc.; page 9, ©Apurva Madia/ Shutterstock, Inc.; page 10, ©Lucian Coman/Shutterstock, Inc.; page 14, ©Olena Mykhaylova/Shutterstock, Inc.; page 19, ©Gorilla/Shutterstock, Inc.; page 20, ©Adrian Britton/Shutterstock, Inc.; page 21, ©Matthew Benoit/Shutterstock, Inc.; page 32, ©Tania McNaboe

Library of Congress Cataloging-in-Publication Data
Rau, Dana Meachen, 1971–
Making butterfly gardens / by Dana Meachen Rau.
p. cm. — (How-to library. Crafts)
Includes bibliographical references and index.
ISBN 978-1-61080-472-1 (lib. bdg.) —
ISBN 978-1-61080-559-9 (e-book) —
ISBN 978-1-61080-646-6 (pbk.)
1. Butterfly gardening—Juvenile literature. I. Title.
QL544.6.R38 2012
638'.5789—dc23   2012011317

Cherry Lake Publishing would like to acknowledge the work of The Partnership for 21st Century Skills. Please visit *www.21stcenturyskills.org* for more information.

Printed in the United States of America
Corporate Graphics Inc.
July 2012
CLFA11

HOW-TO LIBRARY

TABLE OF CONTENTS

Beautiful Bugs

A butterfly is a type of insect.

Have you ever walked through a garden in summer? You may spot lots of colorful flowers. Above your head, it may look like flower petals are flitting in the air, too. But those aren't flowers. They're butterflies! Butterflies dart around gardens. They **alight** on flowers and rocks.

A butterfly is a type of insect. Like other insects, butterflies have three main body segments, six legs, and antennae. Some people consider butterflies to be one of the most beautiful insects because of their two sets of large colorful wings.

Thousands of kinds of butterflies live all over the world. Their wings display many different colors and patterns. Monarchs are some of the most recognizable butterflies. They have orange and black wings. Some butterflies are bright blue. The buckeye has yellow and blue spots. Swallowtails have small "tails" on the ends of their wings. Zebra swallowtails are white with black stripes.

You can invite butterflies to your own yard or outdoor area by creating a butterfly **habitat** for them. Design and plant a garden with flowers to attract these beautiful insects.

BUTTERFLY OR MOTH?
Butterflies and moths look a lot alike. But these insects have a few differences. In general, butterflies have long, slim bodies. Moths are often shorter and fatter. Butterflies are active during the day. Most moths are active at night. Butterflies usually rest with their wings in an upright position. Many moths rest with their wings flat. Butterflies are also usually more colorful.

Life Cycle

Butterflies change a lot during their lives. They go through four stages of growth: egg, larva, pupa, and adult.

Egg

Adult butterflies either lay a single egg or a group of eggs together. They lay their eggs on leaves that their young can eat after hatching.

Larva

The larva, or caterpillar, comes out of an egg. It is tiny and can't travel very far, so it feeds on the plant it hatches on. The caterpillar grows. When its outer layer gets too small, it cracks open and falls off. A caterpillar **molts** four to five times as it grows to full size.

Pupa

When the caterpillar is done eating and growing, it dangles its body from a leaf or branch. Its outer skin splits and breaks off.

SCARING AWAY ENEMIES
Birds and other insects like to eat butterflies. Their bright colors make them easy to see. But this actually keeps them safe. Many butterflies taste bad. So their bright color is a warning. It means "Don't eat me!"

Underneath, its body hardens into a shell called a **chrysalis**. Inside the chrysalis, the caterpillar is changing into a butterfly.

Adult

The chrysalis cracks open when the butterfly is ready. The butterfly's body is soft at first. The butterfly spreads its wings to dry them out. Its body hardens. Then it is ready to fly.

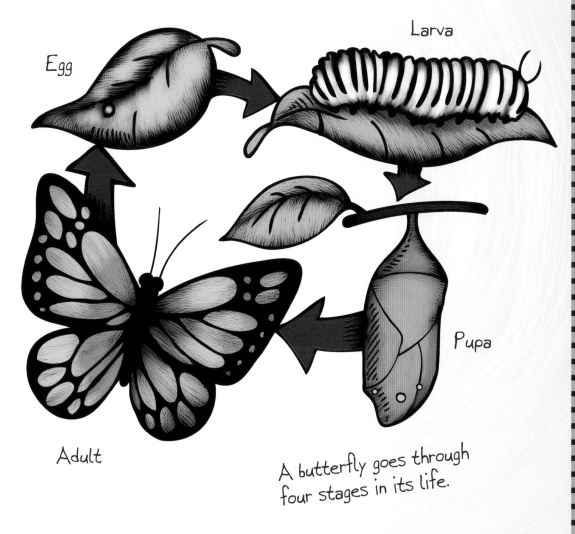

Egg

Larva

Pupa

Adult

A butterfly goes through four stages in its life.

Butterfly Behaviors

Butterflies often alight in fields of flowers.

Before you plant a butterfly garden, find a place to observe butterflies. You might see some in a field, park, wetlands, public garden, or butterfly **conservatory**. Watch their habits.

You might notice a butterfly sitting on a rock. It is **basking** in the sun. Butterflies are cold-blooded. That means they don't have a constant body temperature. They have to depend on the temperature of the air around them. They can't fly if they are too cold. So a butterfly may alight on a flat rock in the sun to warm itself. If the temperature outside is too hot, butterflies will look for a shady spot to rest.

Watch closely as a butterfly lands on a flower. You'll see it uncoil a long tubelike body part that it sticks into the center of the flower. This **proboscis** is like a straw. It sucks **nectar** out of the flower. Nectar is a sweet liquid that gives butterflies energy to fly.

You might also notice a bunch of butterflies gathered together at the edges of a puddle. Besides sucking up nectar, butterflies need salt and other **nutrients**. They can get these by **puddling**—gathering near puddles and sucking up water.

WORKING TOGETHER
Flowers and butterflies help each other. Flowers have the nectar that butterflies drink. Flowers also have pollen. Pollen needs to move from one plant to another so the plant can **reproduce**. Sometimes, pollen sticks to the body of a butterfly. As the butterfly flies from flower to flower, it brings the pollen along for the ride and leaves it behind on the new plant.

Butterflies and flowers need each other.

Welcoming Habitats

Plants need sun, water, and care to grow.

Now that you've gone out to observe butterflies, you can bring the butterflies to you! Create your own butterfly garden in your yard or outdoor space. You can plant a garden in the ground if you have enough room. Plant flowers in pots or window boxes if your space is more limited. A welcoming garden needs:

Nectar flowers

Butterflies are attracted to flowers with strong scents and bright colors. The more types of flowers you plant, the greater variety of butterflies you'll attract.

Host plants

Caterpillars need food, too. Plants that feed new caterpillars are called host plants.

Puddles

Puddles will give adult butterflies the extra nutrients that they can't get from nectar.

Sun and shade

Sunlight helps plants grow. It will also give your butterflies the warmth they need. Place some flat rocks on the ground for basking. Be sure there is also a shady area nearby for days when the temperature is too hot.

Shelter

Butterflies are delicate. They can't handle strong winds. Plant your garden in an area with a windbreak, such as a row of trees or shrubs. These plants will help cut down on wind.

Making a Plan

Snapdragons

Purple Coneflowers

Marigolds

Plan before you plant!

Puddle

You have to do some thinking and planning before you start planting. Here are some questions to ask yourself:

Where is the best place to plant my garden? Check out your possible garden spaces. Look for a spot that gets sun about 8 hours of the day, with nearby shade and little wind.

What size and shape do I want my garden?

The size and shape may depend on the space you have. Start small. Keeping up a garden is a big job. You can always expand your garden once you get the hang of it.

BEST TIME FOR BUTTERFLIES

Butterflies are active year-round in some areas. But in general butterflies are most active in the middle to late summer. Spring is a good time to plant a butterfly garden. Some flowers have a short blooming period, and others have a long one. Be sure to choose plants that will provide nectar for your butterflies throughout the whole season.

What types of plants do I want in my garden?

See pages 14–15 for a list of popular plants that butterflies and caterpillars like. Think about which plants you like, too. Some plants grow taller than others. These might be good in the back of a garden as a windbreak. It is also good to plant the same type of flower in a group. It is easier for butterflies to see a group of flowers than it is for them to see a single flower.

What types of butterflies do I want to attract to my

garden? Depending on where you live, your garden will attract different kinds of butterflies. Research butterflies that are **native** to your area. You can find this information in online resources or a butterfly field guide. These guides will also tell you the right flowers to plant to attract butterflies in your area.

Choosing Plants

The next page lists nectar-producing flowers and host plants that are enjoyed by many types of butterflies and caterpillars. It is not a complete list.

Check gardening guides or online sources to find out if these plants are native to your area. Then visit a garden shop or nursery to buy plants or seeds to start your garden. Read the seed packets or pot labels to find out if the plants grow well in sun or shade, when they bloom, and how far apart to plant them. Look for healthy green plants that are not wilted or dry.

Some plants are **perennials**. This means they bloom for more than one season. If you use them, you won't have to replant your garden every year. **Annuals** are plants that only grow one season. However, they often bloom longer than perennials.

Snapdragons are a good host plant for caterpillars.

Butterflies are attracted to purple coneflowers.

Good plants for butterflies:

Asters

Bee balm

Butterfly bush

Butterfly weed

Goldenrod

Hyssop

Marigolds

Purple coneflowers

Verbena

Zinnias

Good host plants for caterpillars:

Alfalfa

Cottonwood

Milkweed

Mustards

Nettles

Parsley

Pawpaws

Poplar

Snapdragons

Willow

Basic Gardening Tools

Here are the tools you need
to start and keep a successful garden.

For gardening:
- *Shovel or spade*—to dig your garden
- *Garden fork*—to loosen the soil and stir in nutrients
- *Garden rake*—to smooth out the soil
- *Hoe*—to dig rows for seeds
- *Trowel*—to dig holes for plants
- *Pruners or scissors*—to trim plants

For watering:
- *Watering can*—to water specific areas of the garden.
  Watering cans provide a gentle shower that won't flood
  your seeds.
- *Garden hose*—to bring water from the faucet to where you
  need it
- *Spray nozzle*—to attach to your hose to spray water on
  your garden. Use a nozzle that has a gentle spray.
- *Sprinkler*—to attach to the hose to provide a steady rain
  of water on your garden

For yourself:

- *Wheelbarrow*—to help you carry your tools
- *Old clothes*—for when you get down and dirty
- *Garden gloves*—to protect your hands
- *Knee pads*—to protect your knees when kneeling
- *Sunscreen and hat with a brim*—to protect yourself from the sun
- *Water bottle*—to stay hydrated

Gather your supplies and get started!

Digging and Planting

You want to give your flowers the best chance at survival. Take time to prepare the area well.

Digging

If you are digging up part of your yard to make a garden, you'll have to remove the grass first. Push the shovel into the ground at a shallow angle, just under the roots of the grass. Push on the shovel handle like a lever to loosen the roots from the soil. Lift up the patch of grass. Shake the extra soil off the roots so it falls back into the garden. Continue digging the grass from the area until it is clear.

Loosen the soil by scraping the garden fork over the entire garden bed. Remove any rocks. Loose soil makes it easier for plants to send their roots down into the ground.

Your plants also need nutrients to help them grow. Sprinkle **compost** over the area. Compost is a rich mixture of nutrients made from plant matter. Rake it into the soil and smooth out the garden bed.

Planting

If you are planting seeds, dig a shallow trench with the hoe. Look at the back of the seed packets to see how far apart and how deep to plant the seeds. It will be different for every type of flower. Cover the seeds gently with a layer of dirt. Water them to keep them moist.

If you are planting plants, dig a hole with the trowel about the same size as the plant's container. Carefully pull the plant out of the pot. Hold it near the base of its stem so it doesn't break. Loosen the roots and soil of the plant, but try to keep as much of the original soil around it as possible. Place the plant in the hole. Then fill up the rest of the hole with soil and gently pat it around the base. Water the base to give the roots a good drink.

WHEN TO WATER

Water seeds and plants daily when they are newly planted. It is best to water in the early morning and in the evening. Water plants near the base at the soil not just on the top leaves. If it rains, nature does the watering for you. A garden needs about 1 inch (2.5 cm) of water per week throughout the whole growing season.

Remember to water new plants daily.

Keeping It Neat

There is still work to be done as your garden grows. Besides flowers and host plants, you may notice some unwanted plants popping up in your garden. These weeds can take valuable nutrients away from your flowers. You'll need to remove them.

It is easiest to weed right after it has rained and the soil is moist. Grab the weed as close as you can to the base and pull. You want to be sure to get out all the roots. The weed will grow back again if you only pull off the stem or leaves.

Pull out the roots of weeds to prevent them from coming back.

Wood chips help keep weeds from growing.

You can prevent weed growth by **mulching** your garden. Spread a layer of natural material, such as wood chips, dried leaves, or straw over the soil. Mulch also helps keep moisture close to the soil so it doesn't dry out too easily.

Stores sell chemicals to help control weeds. But these chemicals can be harmful to butterflies and other animals. Don't use them on a butterfly garden. Natural mulching and weeding is healthier for butterflies.

Flowers will come and go as your plants bloom. Keep your garden neat by removing dead flower heads. As flowers fade and die, snip them at the base with a pruner or scissors. This helps the plant put more energy into the new flowers waiting to come out.

Permanent Puddle

WELCOME BUTTERFLIES!

Make a welcoming spot for butterflies to stop for a sip.

Make a gathering place for puddling butterflies. They will stop to sip up the nutrients they need.

Materials

Trowel

A clay or plastic plant saucer, about 10 to 16 inches (25 to 41 centimeters) in diameter

Dirt from the garden

Rocks

Watering can

5 wooden craft sticks

Glue

Permanent markers

Fill the saucer with soil.

Steps

1. Choose a sunny spot in your garden. Use the trowel to dig a hole a little wider than your saucer. Place the saucer in the hole. Pat the soil around it so that the saucer is level with the ground.

2. Fill your saucer almost all the way to the top with soil from the garden. Add in a few rocks of various sizes and colors as perches for butterflies.

3. Sprinkle the soil in the saucer with water from the watering can so that the soil is soaked and there is some standing water on the surface.

4. Make a sign to welcome the butterflies. Place four craft sticks flat. Glue the other stick across them. Let the glue dry. Write your message on the front with a marker.

5. Place the sign in the ground near the puddle.

6. Each time you water your garden, soak the soil in your puddle, too.

Make a simple sign with craft sticks and glue.

Fruit Feeder

You can supply your butterfly visitors
with even more sweet food by making
a fruit feeder. This hanging plate reuses
materials you might otherwise throw
away, such as plastic lids, shoelaces,
and overripe fruit.

Materials

Black permanent marker
Large, round, clear lid from a plastic
    take-out or other type of container
Paintbrush
Various colors of acrylic paint
Awl or drill
2 old shoelaces
Scissors
Overripe fruit

Add fruit to this feeder to share a sweet snack with butterflies.

Steps

1. Use the marker to draw a
   flower shape on the top of
   the lid. You could also create
   a design of your own choosing.
   Use a paintbrush to fill in the
   lines of the design with paint.
   Let the paint dry.

Draw and paint a
flower on the lid top.

2. Have an adult poke holes with the
   awl or drill in four spots around the edges of the lid's surface.
3. Cut each shoelace in half. Poke the tip of each lace from
   the underside of the lid up through the top. Tie a knot in
   each one.
4. Flip the lid over. Pull up on all the laces.
   Tie the four ends together in a knot.
5. Hang your feeder on a garden
   hook or the branch of a tree
   overhanging your garden.
   Place overripe fruit, such
   as melon, bananas,
   strawberries, or peaches,
   onto the lid. As the fruit
   dries out, rinse your lid,
   and replace with more fruit
   throughout the butterfly season.

Knot the laces to
secure them to the lid.

Nectar Feeder

Create a flower-shaped feeder filled with nectar.

Butterflies get most of their nectar from flowers. You can also attract them with a feeder filled with homemade sweet nectar.

Materials

1 small container and
  1 medium container
  that fit inside each other
Sheet of craft foam
Pencil
Scissors
Drill
Wooden dowel about 3 to 4 feet
  (1 to 1.2 meters) long
Electrical tape
Colorful stickers
Water and sugar
Plastic scouring pad (in a bright color)

Steps

1. Trace the bottom of the medium container onto the sheet of foam. Draw petal shapes around the circle. Cut out the circle and flower shape from the foam. Set aside.

2. Have an adult drill a hole the same size as your dowel in the bottom of the medium container.

3. Stick the dowel through the hole. Secure it with electrical tape on the bottom and inside of the container.

4. Decorate the outside of the container with colorful stickers.

5. Pull the flower shape onto the container from the bottom so that it fits snugly.

Draw a flower shape on the craft foam.

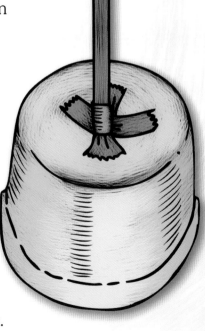

Secure the dowel with electrical tape.

6. Mix up a batch of nectar. The recipe is 4 parts water to 1 part sugar. Have an adult help you boil the water in a small pot on the stove. When it boils, add the sugar. Stir until the sugar disappears. Let the mixture cool completely.

You can make your own nectar with sugar and water.

7. Place the scouring pad in the smaller container. Pour in some of the nectar. You can store the extra nectar for up to a week in the refrigerator.

8. Place the dowel of the feeder into the ground in your garden. Place the small container inside the medium one. The scouring pad will soak up the nectar and be a good perching spot for butterflies.

9. Every few days, remove the small container and rinse the scouring pad and container with warm water. Fill the feeder with fresh nectar.

Watch and Wait

Now that you've created a spot for butterflies, create a spot for yourself. You've worked hard planting such a healthy garden. Place a bench or lawn chair near your new butterfly space and take a seat.

Now it's time to watch and wait. You might start noticing butterflies flitting through the air. Maybe they are looking for nectar to drink. Perhaps they are searching for a safe place to lay eggs. You may notice caterpillars munching on the leaves of your host plants. If you are lucky, you may even see a chrysalis with a new butterfly waiting to emerge.

Keep a notebook close by to create your own field guide. Each time you see a new kind of butterfly, draw a sketch of what it looks like. Write down the flowers it visits and other behaviors. You'll learn a lot about butterflies and how to make the best garden for them.

BUTTERFLY HOUSES
You can buy a wooden butterfly house for your garden, too. The front has small slits that are just big enough for butterflies to slip in and take shelter from the wind and weather.

The holes in a butterfly house are just the right size for these colorful insects.

Glossary

alight (uh-LITE) to land from the air

annuals (AN-yoo-uhlz) plants that grow one season

basking (BASS-king) warming in the sun

chrysalis (KRIS-uh-lis) the case that encloses the butterfly during the pupa stage

compost (KAHM-pohst) a rich mixture of nutrients made from plant matter

compound (KAHM-pound) having more than one part

conservatory (kuhn-SURV-uh-tor-ee) a building with a glass roof and walls to let in sun

habitat (HAB-uh-tat) an animal's home in nature

molts (MOHLTS) sheds old skin

mulching (MUL-ching) spreading a layer of natural material over soil to prevent weed growth

native (NAY-tiv) found naturally in a certain area

nectar (NEK-tur) a sweet liquid produced by flowers that butterflies drink for energy

nutrients (NOO-tree-uhnts) the food plants and animals need to grow and be healthy

perennials (puh-REN-ee-uhlz) plants that grow for multiple seasons

proboscis (pruh-BAHSS-kiss) the body part that a butterfly uses to drink nectar

puddling (PUHD-ling) the butterfly behavior of gathering near puddles

reproduce (ree-pruh-DOOS) make more of

For More Information

Books

Aston, Dianna Hutts. *A Butterfly Is Patient*. San Francisco: Chronicle Books, 2011.

Knudsen, Shannon. *Eggs, Legs, Wings: A Butterfly Life Cycle*. Mankato, MN: Capstone Press, 2011.

Koontz, Robin Michal. *Composting: Nature's Recyclers*. Minneapolis: Picture Window Books, 2007.

Simon, Seymour. *Butterflies*. New York: Collins, 2011.

Stewart, Melissa. *A Place for Butterflies*. Atlanta: Peachtree Publishers, 2006.

Web Sites

The Butterfly Website

http://butterflywebsite.com

Play games and watch videos of butterflies in action.

Missouri Botanical Garden: Butterfly House

www.missouribotanicalgarden.org/visit/family-of-attractions /butterfly-house.aspx

Check out pictures and learn more about different kinds of butterflies.

Organic Gardening: Butterfly Gardening

www.organicgardening.com/learn-and-grow/butterfly-gardening

Read some tips for attracting more butterflies to your garden.

Index

About the Author

Dana Meachen Rau is the author of more than 300 books for children on many topics, including science, history, cooking, and crafts. She creates, experiments, researches, and writes from her home office in Burlington, Connecticut.